NI 11/21

C(.)

West Sussex County Council Library

Please return/renew this item by the last
date shown. Books may also be renewed
by phone 01243 642110 or the Internet.

www.westsussex.gov.uk

west
sussex
county
council

A FOCUS ON...

DISABILITY

By
John Wood

©2018
Book Life
King's Lynn
Norfolk PE30 4LS

ISBN: 978-1-78637-217-8

Written by:
John Wood

Edited by:
Kirsty Holmes

Designed by:
Evie Wright

A catalogue record for this book
is available from the British Library

PHOTO CREDITS

**Abbreviations: l-left, r-right, b-bottom,
t-top, c-centre, m-middle.**

Front cover – Denis Kuvaev. 2 – wavebreakmedia. 3 – StockSmartStart. 4 – sweetmonster. 5 – martin bowra. 6c – Michaelpuche. 6r – Eleonora_os. 7 – Jaromir Chalabala. 8 – Francesco83. 9l – a2l. 9r – Shchipkova Elena. 10 – goodluz. 11 – GUNDAM_Ai. 12 – Mila Supinskaya Glashchenko. 13 – wikimedia. 14 – Sergey Nivens. 15 – wavebreakmedia. 16 – Em7. 17 –sippakorn. 18 – Khrystofor. 19 – Andrey Armyagov. 20 – Rova N. 21 –Vladislav Gajic. 22 –wavebreakmedia. 23 – StockSmartStart

Images are courtesy of Shutterstock.com.
With thanks to Getty Images, Thinkstock Photo and iStockphoto.

DISABILITY

Words that look **like** this can be found in the glossary on page 24.

What Is a Disability?

When a part of someone's brain or body doesn't work the way it should, it might affect their ability to do certain things. This is called a disability.

This boy has a disability called cerebral palsy.

Disabilities can be very difficult, **continuous** problems for the people that have them. When someone has a disability, it usually means they have to do a few things differently.

Different Types of Disability

There are all sorts of different disabilities. Sometimes we can see them and sometimes we can't. Sometimes a person can have more than one disability.

Some people are born with disabilities. Some people become disabled after a serious accident or illness.

Movement

Some disabilities make it hard or impossible to walk, stand or move around.

"The doctor says my spine doesn't work properly. This means I can't feel my legs, so I use a wheelchair like this one every day".

Natalie – aged 8

Some staircases have lifts that can carry wheelchairs upstairs. There are also different toilets which are easier to use if someone has this kind of disability.

Accessible **Toilets**

Wheelchair Lift

Seeing and Hearing

Some people can't see. People who can't see are said to be blind, or **partially** blind.

"My mum has a guide dog and a long stick to help her walk around because she can't see." Matilda – aged 5

Hearing Aid

Some people have a hearing disability. When someone can't hear what people are saying well enough to understand them, we say they are deaf.

Disability and Sports

Being in a wheelchair doesn't mean you can't move around quickly. There are lots of sports played by people in wheelchairs, like rugby and basketball.

This man plays wheelchair basketball.

There are sports for people with other disabilities too.

Blind Football

"My disability means I can't see. When I grow up, I want to be a footballer."

Hidden Disabilities

Some disabilities can't be seen because they **affect** the brain. People with hidden disabilities might find it hard to get the help they need. This is because other people can't see their disability straight away.

Dyslexia is a hidden disability. It can mean people have trouble reading words and letters in the right order.

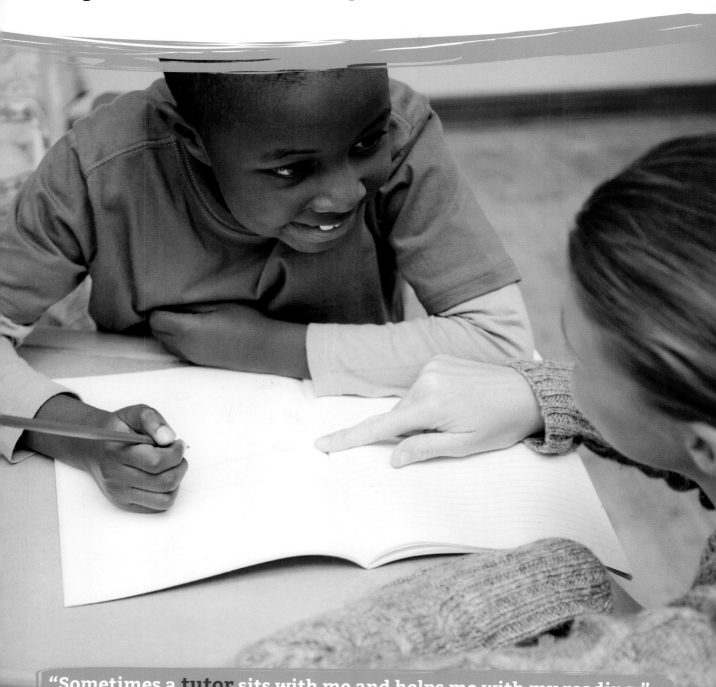

"Sometimes a **tutor** sits with me and helps me with my reading."

Nicholas – aged 7

Autism

Autism is another hidden disability. People with autism often find it hard to understand other people, or to tell others how they feel.

TODAY

9:00 School

11:00 Sensory room

1:00 Lunch

2:00 Play outside

3:00 Home time

Some people with autism like to plan their day so they know exactly what is going to happen.

Being autistic means you see the world in a different way.
Some sounds or lights can feel too much for people with autism.

"My autism makes some sounds seem very loud and some colours seem very bright. My teachers help me when I feel like this."

Anita – aged 7

Learning

Some disabilities, like Down's syndrome, can affect someone's **ability** to learn. People with a disability like this find it harder to learn things at school.

This girl has Down's syndrome.

Down's syndrome is a disability that people have from birth.

"My sister has Down's syndrome. We play together all the time.

She especially likes to go swimming."

Raj – aged 6

Understanding Disabilities

It can be difficult to live with a disability. Some disabilities might make it hard to open doors, read a book or say the right thing.

This sign points out things that help disabled people, like bus seats or parking spaces.

If someone finds something difficult, we should always try to help them.

'My friend has a hearing disability. When we play games in the playground, I always make sure she understands the rules because she can't hear as well."

Louise – aged 6

Living with a Disability

You might have a disability or know someone that does. Having a disability is hard, but it doesn't mean you can't do everyday things like going to school and playing with friends.

A disability is only one part of someone's life. We are all different in one way or another. The important thing is to learn about these differences together.

GLOSSARY

ability	how well we are able to do something
accessible	easier to use for someone with a disability
accident	something bad that happens by chance
affect	to make a difference to something
cerebral palsy	a disability which affects movement and muscle control, caused by a problem in the brain from birth
continuous	something that keeps going
partially	partly, or only in some ways
spine	the bones in your centre of your back that help you stand up
tutor	a teacher who usually teaches one or a few pupils

INDEX